MIDLAND
IN THE
WESTERN MIDLANDS

Compiled by D. R. HARVEY

WEST MIDLANDS TRANSPORT IN PICTURES

A
BTHG
PUBLICATION

ISBN 0 905103 11 4

© 1990

Published by Birmingham Transport Historical Group,
43 Beauchamp Avenue, Birmingham B20 1DR.
Printed by W. J. Ray & Co. Ltd., Warewell Street, Walsall, West Midlands WS1 2HQ.

1377 [HA 8004]
The first Midland "Red" double-deckers after the solid-tyred FSs of 1923 were the fifty one R.E.D.D.s built in 1932 and 1933. However, even these were unusual in that the body building contract was split between Metro-Cammell (M.C.C.W.), Short Bros. of Rochester, Brush and Eastern Counties. The M.C.C.W. buses were a fairly early example of all-metal bodies built to a non-standard design, in this case specifically to B.M.M.O.'s requirements. This is 1377, a Short Bros. bodied example, seen at Great Malvern on the long 144 route in 1938. This Birmingham based bus was soon to be transferred to Coalville in Leicestershire and remained in service until 1949.   (R. Wilson)

COVER PHOTOGRAPH

2336 [FHA 840] & 4407 [VHA 407]
The terminus for a number of services in Birmingham was in Station Street which ran on the southern side of New Street Station from Hill Street to Worcester Street. It was often congested with too many buses competing for too few parking spaces. This busy 1958 scene was probably a Bank Holiday, judging from the amount of activity. 2336 is working a 198 service to Tamworth via Curdworth. 4407, a M.C.C.W. bodied B.M.M.O. D7 had let its passengers disembark in the middle of the road, while just visible is a D5 on the 147 route to Astwood Bank.   (A. B. Cross)

2

FOREWORD

The photographs of Midland Red vehicles depicted in the volume not only portray the evolution of the Company's fleet from the late 1920s and the early '30s to the 1950s but also provide an interesting impression of the contemporary street and social scene.

They cover a period when Birmingham and the Midlands were beginning to come to grips with the motor age. Even in the early 1930s the volume of traffic, it is said, threatened to strangle the flow of goods on the city's main arterial roads and in fact it was not until 1955 — towards the end of the period covered by these photographs — that the dual carriageway from Deritend to Digbeth was opened.

Notwithstanding the growth of private motoring the number of passengers carried by the company continued to rise until 1954, thereafter a decline began caused by the rising costs of fuel and labour which were reflected in higher fares. Bus traffic was also diminished by increasing car ownership and the advent of television.

However, in developing its fleet to provide for its passengers' requirements the Birmingham and Midland Motor Omnibus Company, to give the firm its full name, was certainly to the fore in engineering terms. This is well exemplified by the productions from its workshops of the four SOS rear engined coaches in 1935, the motorway coach of 1959 and the D10 underfloor engined double decker of 1960.

In this period, the industry could still command general appeal as evidenced by the extensive use made of its services and the interest shown in its activities by the general public. Indeed, the *Eagle* comic published detailed drawings and technical information of the motorway coach of 1959 for its young readers.

Although the attractions of private motoring have already been noted, the streets depicted in these illustrations certainly do not contain evidence of the congestions which plague the industry today. Thus in many respects these were the halcyon years of achievement and service when the bus played its most dominant rôle in the transport scene of the Midlands.

As a previous general manager of the Company, I was always conscious of the pride which those who worked for the Company rightly had in its many achievements and its striving to give good service.

This book well depicts Midland Red during its heyday when it operated nearly 2,000 vehicles, employed approximately 8,000 staff and justly earned the name of the Friendly Midland Red!

John A. Birks,
Abingdon, Oxon.

ACKNOWLEDGEMENTS

The Birmingham Transport Historical Group wishes to thank all the photographers who have contributed to this volume; their work is acknowledged beneath each caption. However, special thanks go to Alan B. Cross and Robert Humm for access to the photographic collections of the late Bob Mack and S. N. J. White respectively, and to Alan Broughall whose many unusual photographs feature in this volume.

The compiler also gratefully acknowledges the help given to him by members of the B.T.H.G., particularly Paul Addenbrooke and Peter Hale.

Further credit must also be given to Barry Ware, whose advice and informative comments helped enormously in the compilation of this album.

Finally, thanks must go to Mrs. Diana Harvey, for typing the manuscript.

INTRODUCTION

This compilation of photographs continues the Birmingham Transport Historical Group's series West Midlands Transport in Pictures. It covers a thirty year period, starting with vehicles which were introduced in the late 1920s. These opened up new areas and routes and effectively replaced many local tram services, particularly in the Black Country, by fast, reliable, lightweight buses. The photographs show how the Birmingham and Midland Motor Omnibus Company (B.M.M.O.) developed its own effective yet idiosyncratic style throughout the 1930s. Revolutionary engineering changes continued during that period and eventually resulted in the fleet of underfloor engined single-deckers of the late 1940s. This culminated in the late 1950s with chassisless double-deckers and coaches capable of sustained motorway journeys at high speed.

The photographs cover an area that is loosely based on the Western Midlands. It concentrates on Birmingham and the towns of the West Midlands conurbation which make up the Black Country, but also covers Stafford, Burton, Lichfield to the North, Coventry to the East, Leamington to the South East, Worcester, Malvern and Hereford to the South West and Bridgnorth to the West.

The selection of photographs is intended to show all aspects of Midland "Red" operation in time, in place and in varied circumstances, using photographs which generally have not been previously published.

David Harvey,
October, 1990.   Dudley, West Midlands.

GLOSSARY

The Midland "Red" Company did not introduce a sequential system of fleet numbering until 1944; prior to that buses were known by their registration numbers. For the sake of consistency, the allocated fleet number has been used on all photographs, including those taken before 1944.

Listed below are the abbreviations used in the text by Midland "Red" to describe their vehicles.

BRR	— Bus Rolls-Royce.
C	— postwar coach.
CON	— Converted ON.
D	— Postwar double-decker.
DON	— Diesel Onward. (A.E.C. engine).
FEDD	— Front Entrance Double-Decker.
IM	— Improved Madam.
K type	— B.M.M.O. Kidney 8.028 direct injection Diesel/oil engine, so called because of the shape of the combustion chambers within the engine.
M	— Madam.
MM	— Modified Madam.
OLR	— Open Rolls-Royce.
ON	— Onward.
ONC	— Onward Coach.
Q	— Queen.
QL	— Queen Low.
REDD	— Rear Entrance Double-Decker.
S	— postwar single-decker bus.
SLR	— Saloon Low Rolls-Royce.
SON	— Saloon Onward.
SOS	— reputedly meaning "Shire's Own Specification".
XL	— EXceL.

337 [HA 2250]
Standing in a Bearwood side street in the late 1940s is HA 2250. This Tilling-Stevens FS was originally built in 1923 with a Carlyle O22/29F double-deck body. When Midland "Red" suspended double-deck operation in 1928 this bus was fitted with a 'Q' type 4.344 litre petrol engine and an 'S' type single-deck body. Three years later the bus was equipped for dual control training and given a full front. In this guise it lasted until 1952. It was based at Bearwood garage for use by the Central Driving School and was regularly seen in Bearwood and Smethwick. Many Midland "Red" drivers had their initation into the art of double declutching on this splendid veteran.

(S. E. Letts)

923 [HA 4848]
Parked on the forecourt of Bearwood garage are two veterans of the fleet which survived into postwar days. The nearer bus is 923, a 1928 Q.L. with a Ransomes B37F body built in 1928. These were the first S.O.S. vehicles to feature four wheel brakes. The other bus is 1060 whose complicated early history is indicated only by the unusual radiator style. It is a six cylinder M.M. type but had originally been built as an XL coach in 1929. These were overweight and unstable and within a year all were rebodied by Ransomes, Sims & Jefferies. 1060 outlived 923 by just one year, being withdrawn in 1950.

(A. D. Broughall)

5

906 [HA 4838]
In 1928 B.M.M.O. introduced the Q.L. type and nearly one hundred and seventy of them were built between 1928 and 1929. Most of the bodies of this class were built by Brush and seated thirty seven passengers. These vehicles were among the last to have a rocker-panel style of body and were the first S.O.S. buses to have equal-sized wheels all-round. 906 is in Bearwood about 1950. It was withdrawn from service three years earlier and is being used as a driver trainer. As a safety precaution for the trainee and the instructor, the fuel tank was removed from beneath the driver's seat!
(S. N. J. White)

XL Class]
The driver and conductor pose in front of this unidentified XL type in Coventry in 1930. This class of 42 coaches was destined to see about one year's service in original condition, as the bodies were too heavy for the six cylinder, five litre petrol engine. The vehicles were very modern for their time, incorporating a neat, rounded radiator which was a vast improvement on the previous multi-barrelled design. Fitted with luxurious seating and an outward-opening door, it is about to go to Leicester via Wolvey, Sharnford and Narborough.
(R. Wilson)

1312 [HA 6242]
Throughout the early postwar years, some fairly elderly vehicles lingered on in service. This is 1312 a 1931 IM6 with a Brush B34F body which had run on producer gas in 1943. It is in Steelhouse Lane passing Birmingham City Transport tramcar 710, which was to last in service until 1953. HA 6242 is being used on driver training in this 1950 view and was to see service for another two years. (A. B. Cross)

1314 [HA 6244]
S.O.S. IM6 1314 stands awaiting its driver outside the Scala Cinema in Angel Place, Worcester. The feature film helps to date this scene at about 1938. The chassis was built in 1931, although the body dated from 1930 and was from a COD 4 chassis. It saw service for twenty years, despite being impressed for two years by the War Department. Many buses on their return from such use were often in so poor a state that they did not re-enter service. On its return to Midland "Red", 1314 ran in khaki livery from 1943 to 1945. (R. Wilson)

7

Sutton Garage
Sutton garage was opened on 26 August 1934 with a capacity for sixty vehicles within the brick four bay frontage. However, for the first four years of operation, Sutton's local services were restricted to single-deck vehicles as the local council would not allow double-deck operation in the town. Along with 1437 [HA 8313] and 1444 [HA 8320], both 1933 IM6s with Short B34F bodies, and 1363 [HA 8288], a 1932 IM4 with a Brush body, is 1585 [HA 9450], a F.E.D.D. of 1934 with a typical Brush fifty-six seater body.   (R. Wilson)

1483 [HA 9380]
Opposite the Thimblemill baths in Smethwick is 1483, a 1934 B.R.R. with a Short B34F body. These buses had rather exaggeratedly deep roofs, which emphasised the lack of destination boxes and placed the stencil route number in the dark recess of the canopy. This early postwar view shows the rather basic front wings. 1483 still has, as a remnant of its war service, one of the small headlights which were standard fittings when the larger originals had to be replaced. 1483 was to continue with Midland "Red" until 1952. This gave the bus an eighteen year service life, which was considerably longer than the buses which replaced it.   (D. R. Harvey collection)

8

1512 [HA 9472]
Birmingham's Cannon Hill Park is not usually associated as a Midland "Red" terminus so this 1934 O.N. 1512 may have been on a private hire. This vehicle's original petrol engine was replaced with the 'K' type eight litre Diesel engine in 1937 and was therefore reclassified as a C.O.N. type. The 27 feet 6 inches long Short Bros. body seated thirty eight passengers in a body style which introduced a moulded waistrail and the hint of a destination box bulge in the front of the dome, a feature not fitted to the prewar single-deckers. This particular bus was rebuilt by Nudd Brothers and Lockyer in 1949 and had its half drop windows replaced by sliding ventilators. Just visible behind is 3697 [NHA 697], a 1950 Brush bodied S10.   (S. N. J. White)

1537 [HA 9402]
The first fifty of the 1934 batch of F.E.D.D.s were bodied by Short's, the seaplane manufacturer. They were constructed in 1934 and had H30/26F bodies. HA 9402 is seen in Sutton Coldfield town centre in about 1938. This splendidly-painted example carries, just above the rear registration plate, its garage identification 'leopard spot' and unusually, a second spot showing that the bus is on loan from another garage. At the extreme nearside bottom rear, a Hackney carriage licence plate is also carried. The rear destination board was another chore for the conductor to remember.   (R. Wilson)

9

1556 [HA 9420]
This 1934 Short Brothers bodied F.E.D.D. is in Navigation Street in early postwar years, waiting for passengers on the 124 route. Here, Midland "Red" had to compete for road space with B.C.T. trams and buses. HA 9420 is still carrying the prewar livery, but has lost its S.O.S. markings which were just below the word 'Midland' on the radiator header tank. Mr. D. M. Sinclair apparently had an aversion to these letters after he became General Manager and all S.O.S. types lost their marque badges. The buildings behind the bus are still in existence, but the shops and offices beside it, were demolished in about 1965.   (J. E. Cull)

1591 [BHA 1]
Chief Engineer L. G. Wyndham Shire designed four rear-engined single-deckers in the 1935-6 period. Although very advanced, they were not altogether successful. Shire's successor, Donald Sinclair, used the design concepts of underfloor engines he had pioneered with Northern General in rebuilding all four. 1591 was the first to be rebuilt in 1941 with a 'K' type oil engine and a German ZF 'Aphon' gearbox. This very advanced vehicle was a most curious mixture of 1930s body styles, reminiscent of N.G.T. SE4 types and London Transport's A.E.C. Q's combining to produce an extremely strange-looking vehicle. It is seen here at Hagley Road West, Bearwood in front of Lightwoods Park.
(S. E. Letts)

1602 [AHA 497]
1602 stands at Six Ways, Erdington, after working the short S67 route from New Oscott. It is a 1934 Short Bros. bodied O.N. which was one of only twelve of the class of fifty that were converted to C.O.N. type in 1938. This postwar view shows the rather severe way in which Carlyle Works had rebuilt the bodies with unradiused windows, sliding ventilators and all-metal sides. On reflection, it seems a shame that the Midland "Red" rebuilds lacked the flair of the original designs, but this must be measured against the urgent need for buses in the early postwar years.
(A. D. Broughall)

1677 [AHA 622]
This vehicle started life as a normal control canvas roof touring coach with a Short Brothers body. Ten years earlier it might have been seen on a week's tour to Devon or Scotland. Such luxury could not be justified when buses were in short supply and 1677 was one of the twenty five O.L.R. types to be converted to a bus in 1941. This gave these 1935 built vehicles the most modern looking frontal aspect of all prewar Midland "Red" buses. They worked out the remainder of their lives in the Birmingham and Black Country areas. This view is taken at the terminus outside Acocks Green library with the bus working the short suburban route to Yardley. (D. Barlow)

1681 [AHA 626]
1681 has been parked beneath the advertising hoardings for Ekco electrical goods, Horlicks and Silver Shred marmalade, while lying over in Railway Drive, Wolverhampton, in 1950. It has come from Kidderminster via the picturesque village of Kinver on the 883 route. The extensively rebuilt, formerly normal control O.L.R. has gold lining-out, which highlighted the rich red livery. Within a year AHA 626 was withdrawn after ten years in its rebuilt form.
(A. B. Cross)

1746 [BHA 305] & 3500 [MHA 500]
The twilight of the careers of Stan Laurel and Oliver Hardy was marked by a most successful tour of England during the early part of 1952. On May 5 1952, they came to the Birmingham Hippodrome and the billboards in Navigation Street advertise their appearance. 1746, one of the F.E.D.D.s with metal-framed M.C.C.W. bodies, stands under the advertisement while working the 130 route to Stourbridge. It, too, was in the twilight of its career and destined to last only another three years. Just visible is B.M.M.O. D5 3500 of 1949 which had a fourteen-year operational life with Midland "Red". (S. N. J. White)

1802 [BHA 346]
This splendid view of 1802 [BHA 346] in Dudley bus station was taken in about 1953. Despite being converted in 1943 to run with an A.E.C. 7.7 litre Diesel engine, the basic design of the F.E.D.D.s was left unaltered. The asymmetrical positioning of the radiator to the nearside contributed to a rather antiquated appearance. Inside the front dome, next to the small side windows, was the front four-seater bench where the whole family could sit in comfort and get the best views of the road ahead. (A. D. Broughall)

1841 [BHA 400]
1841, a 1936 M.C.C.W. bodied S.O.S. F.E.D.D., is parked on the cobbles of Station Street in Birmingham, adjacent to the rear of New Street Station. The advertisement across the rear emergency door remarks: "Banish Parking Headaches! by using the friendly Midland "Red". The last phrase was used as a slogan by the company for many years. This bus is painted in an all-over red livery with some yellow lining-out beneath the lower saloon windows and has received the postwar 'Midland' style of fleetname. Despite its apparent good condition, 1841 is near the end of its service life and is being used as a tuition bus.
(R. F. Mack)

1876 [BHA 835]
The last of the BHA registered F.E.D.D.s was 1876. It is seen working the 315 route which went from Stourbridge to Worcester via Kidderminster. These all-metal M.C.C.W. bodied double-deckers were not rebuilt in postwar years and retained the Midland "Red" 'style' until their withdrawal. This particular bus was re-engined with a 'K' type Diesel in 1944 and was withdrawn in 1954.
(A. B. Cross)

14

1909 [CHA 533]
The S.O.N. with an English Electric body is parked in Gibbins Road, Selly Oak and was, for a few years after sale, regularly seen outside the owner's house. 1909 was withdrawn in 1955 and, unlike many other S.O.N. buses from the CHA batch, was not sold to a showman. The body was extensively rebuilt by Nudd Brothers and Lockyer of Kegworth in 1950 in their typical style, being fitted with rubber-mounted windows and sliding ventilators. The cab structure usually remained unrebuilt, often giving the impression that the rest of the body came from a different bus. (A. D. Broughall)

1943 [CHA 2]
The B.M.M.O. S3 underfloor-engined prototype, 1943, had been rebuilt from the 1936 rear-engined experimental single-decker and had received the body frame from CHA 3. This complicated rebuilding was to create a virtually new vehicle with many characteristics of the postwar S type single-deckers. CHA 2 was remarkable in that it displayed few of the utilitarian features associated with vehicles built at this time. It was also the only S type prototype to feature a Wilson preselector gearbox. It was modified by having a recessed driver's windscreen (as shown here) and a postwar style of destination box. It is seen in Warwick in about 1948. (A. A. Cooper)

15

1996 [CHA 978]
The partially glazed, bomb-damaged roof arches of New Street Station tower over 1996, a 1937 S.L.R. with an English Electric (E.E.C.) C30F body. When new, these full-fronted coaches were at the forefront of modern coach body styling. The tapered pillars were an E.E.C. characteristic on Midland "Reds". To the modern eye, perhaps, the broken level waistrail is a less than pleasing design feature, but it reflected the 1930s vogue developed by other coach builders such as Harrington. CHA 978 is parked in Queens Drive, Birmingham. The class was withdrawn in 1955 and many of them were exported to either Cyprus or the Canary Islands.   (A. B. Cross)

2103 [DHA 721]
Parked in a remote part of Pool Meadow bus station, Coventry, on 21/4/1956 is 2103. This is a S.O.N. with an E.E.C. B38F body. These single-deckers had tapered window pillars and fuel tanks mounted on the offside rather than under the driver's seat. When new, they were painted in the style of the S.L.R. coaches with tapering brown flashes along each side. 2103 was to be withdrawn later in 1956, and in common with this 1937 batch of E.E.C. bodies, was not rebuilt. With the addition of some extra external strapping on the pillar over the rear wheel arch, this single-decker remained largely unchanged throughout its nineteen year service life.   (B. W. Ware)

2116 [DHA 734] & 3207 [JHA 807]
The Georgian Market Place in the County Town of Warwick has always been the focus of Midland "Red" services in the town. The town's bus services were included in the "L" group of Leamington town services until quite recently. This 1950 view shows E.E.C. bodied S.O.N. 2116 working the L41 route and 3207, a one year old B.M.M.O. S8 with a M.C.C.W. body, working the L44 route. The newer bus was extended by two feet six inches to thirty feet length in 1952. This increased its seating capacity by four. The following year, the S.O.N. was withdrawn. (A. B. Cross)

2122 [EHA 254] & 2037 [DHA 655]
Were it not for a keen eye for detail this view might have been taken in prewar days. In fact, 2122, a 1938 Brush bodied F.E.D.D., had been rebuilt in the lower saloon area by Hooton in 1950. It almost retains its prewar appearance, unlike the later utilities which were altered almost beyond rocognition. 2122 is in New Street, Birmingham, about 1951, outside the Arden Hotel. It is in front of 2037, a S.O.N. with an E.E.C. B38F body of 1937 vintage. The buildings behind the buses survived the bombing which devastated New Street on 10 April 1941, but succumbed to demolition in the late 1960s. (S. N. J. White)

2128 [EHA 260]
The Midland "Red"/Stratford Blue noticeboard proclaims, rather unusually, that a "Chauffeur driven luxurious Pullman limousine" was available. This service was offered by Stratford Blue. In the early postwar period bus services, such as the rural 524 route to Evesham, via Broadway, were still requiring the use of double-deckers. Here, at the Red Lion bus station, Stratford-upon-Avon, towards the end of its career is 2128, still with its original radiator. It was one of fifty Brush bodied F.E.D.D.s delivered in 1938. In the background is a Harrington bodied Leyland "Royal Tiger", lying over after bringing visitors to Stratford.   (A. D. Broughall)

2129 [EHA 261]
An extremely smart-looking 2129 of Stourbridge garage arrives at Clent with a short-working on the 318 (Stourbridge and Bromsgrove) service. The overtaking Austin A35 car is about 1957 vintage, which suggests that the bus has only a year or two until its withdrawal in 1960.   (A. B. Cross)

2161 [EHA 293]
St. Georges Parade, near Cleveland Road, Wolverhampton, with its early 19th century buildings, was rarely used for bus routes. 2161 is seen parked here awaiting its next turn of duty. The sunny day and its very dusty appearance suggest that the last few days of operation have been a little arduous. This batch of EHA registered F.E.D.D.s was unique among the 336 of this type that were constructed between 1934 and 1940 as they had their fuel tanks placed in the conventional position outside the chassis frame rather than below the driver's seat. Yet again, a certain amount of rebuilding had taken place on this vehicle and it was to survive in service until 1957.
(S. N. J. White)

2213 [EHA 781]
Careful study of the unrebuilt E.E.C. body on S.O.N. 2213 reveals a certain degree of waistrail sag, suggesting that all was not quite as it should have been beneath the surface. Similar testimony to its age lies in the slightly down at front appearance of its front springs. It is in the part of Station Street, Birmingham, that was swept away in the early 1960s when the Bull Ring Centre, itself now under threat of demolition, was built. EHA 781 stands between two postwar single deckers, one being 3621, bound for more distant parts of the system.
(S. N. J. White)

19

2231 [FHA 213]
The later classes of F.E.D.D. double-deckers had a remarkably long innings, some forty of them lasting until 1960. The memory of these fine vehicles is clouded by the passage of time, but one day they seemed to be working as hard as ever and the next they were gone. This is 2231, one of the 1939 Brush bodied examples which lasted until the end. They were of composite construction and extensively rebuilt, in this case in 1951. Their comparatively unusual forward entrance layout, which other operators claimed caused bulkhead stress and shortened lives, was not apparently a problem. This late 1950s view shows 2231 travelling along Stratford Road towards Birmingham.   (A. B. Cross)

2236 [FHA 218]
The conductress has begun to walk across Birmingham Road from Bromsgrove garage to start her duty on 2236, a 1939 F.E.D.D. with a Brush H30/26F body. It was the practice for crews to change over here when working the long Birmingham-Worcester-Malvern route. The scheduling of the first half of the run was very tight and any crew change at Bromsgrove had to be done swiftly as the next stop was Bromsgrove High Street, where a lot of passenger exchange could take place. On the wall of the garage is the rather dignified company plaque.
(A. B. Cross)

2257 [FHA 239]
The area bounded by Walsall, Wolverhampton and Wednesbury was always something of a 'closed shop' as far as Midland "Red" was concerned. The municipal operators of Walsall and Wolverhampton had operated both trams and trolleybuses in the area and this left Midland "Red" very little scope to infill. One service oddity was the isolated 277 route, which ran between Willenhall and Darlaston, a distance of barely two miles. The route was operated by Wolverhampton garage. On a very un-August looking day in 1955, the driver and conductress have a brief conversation before leaving Willenhall yet again on 2257, a 1939 F.E.D.D. with a Brush H30/26F body.
(D. R. Harvey collection)

2277 [FHA 409]
Another rainy day in Blackpool! 2277, one of twenty-five 1939 Duple bodied O.N.C. were developed from the S.L.R. type of two years earlier. Their sleeker lines and modern appearance kept some of them in front line service until 1960. FHA 409, still with a few years service left, stands in Rigby Road coach station, Blackpool with vehicles belonging to Crosville. The journey back to Kidderminster would have been very relaxing as the O.N.C. class was fitted with an overdrive gearbox to ensure smooth and quiet running on long journeys. (H. Peers)

2295 [FHA 450] & 2299 [FHA 454]
Standing withdrawn are four of the FHA registered S.O.N.s with Brush bodies built in 1939. They were parked in the yard of Hereford garage during late 1958, their withdrawal precipitated by the final deliveries of B.M.M.O. S14 single-deckers. The date is 16/5/1959 and so this forlorn line-up of buses had been standing for several months, testified by the missing headlights on two of the vehicles. They were almost certainly going to be doomed to the scrapyard.   (B. W. Ware)

2305 [FHA 460]
Passengers queue to board 2305, one of the penultimate batch of 1939 S.O.N.s. The 'new look' Christian Dior-styled dress one of the young women is wearing dates the view at about 1951. The Brush-bodied single-decker had been rebuilt by Nudd Bros. & Lockyer in 1950 and in the process lost much of the body's prewar style and panache. The vehicle is loading in Cleveland Road, Wolverhampton, better known as the location of the Corporation's bus and trolleybus depot than for being a major town terminus for Midland "Red". (S. N. J. White)

2306 [FHA 461]
The 314 route ran from Worcester via Ombersley and Stourport to Bewdley, for much of the route running on the east bank of the picturesque valley of the River Severn. The driver of 2306 looks carefully to his left before hauling his prewar S.O.N. single-decker out of Worcester bus station. In the days before power steering, drivers had to develop the correct 'push and pull' technique when making sharp turns. The combination of heavy steering, vacuum brakes and crash gearboxes made the job of bus driving a highly skilled occupation. The conductor had to remember to collect a destination board from the garage for every route that the bus was to cover on that tour of duty.   (D. R. Harvey collection)

2308 [FHA 463]
Standing in Benacre Street yard is S.O.N. 2308, which was one of the last prewar single-deckers to remain in service. This yard was waste land which lay behind Bristol Street, and was flanked by some of the earliest Victorian terraces to be built in Birmingham. The parking of buses in the open was because Digbeth garage did not have the capacity to house all its vehicles. Space was particularly short after the parking facility at the front of the garage was removed when the road was rebuilt as a dual carriageway in the mid 1950s. Benacre Street itself was redeveloped under a new housing scheme in 1965 and its site is difficult to find today.   (A. B. Cross)

2343 [FHA 847]
It was definitely a case of the geriatric helping the young, when one of Bearwood garage's B.M.M.O. D7s broke down while working the B87 route from Birmingham to Dudley via Oldbury. Bearwood garage normally had its own recovery vehicle but, for some reason, 2243, a 1939 Brush bodied F.E.D.D., which was nearing the end of its normal service life, was sent out to bring in the failed unidentifiable newer bus. It appears that the tow is being undertaken with the aid of a rope through the open central rear emergency door of the F.E.D.D.!

(A. D. Broughall)

2345 [FHA 849]
As the distant Walsall Corporation Leyland was built in 1951 and the 1939 F.E.D.D. had not been rebuilt by Hooton until 1951, then one can assume that this view in Walsall bus station dates from about this time. 2345 awaits its driver before returning, via the Scott Arms, to Birmingham via a proposed Walsall Corporation tram route extension of 1901 by which it had been hoped to reach Perry Barr. The F.E.D.D. parked behind the leading vehicle shows subtle differences in the body rebuilding.

(R. Wilson)

24

2352 [FHA 856]
The open bonnet side suggests the worst. The crew are apparently discussing what to do next with their ailing bus. This had happened at the Londonderry pub in Warley. Not being served by any of the Black Country tram companies, the Warley area, to the west of Birmingham, was covered by an extensive system of bus routes by Midland "Red" developed when the housing estates of the area were built in the 1920s. 2352 was one of the many Brush bodied F.E.D.D.s which had only their lower saloons rebuilt. The bus shows the Company's method of putting two lines of wording onto a single destination display. (A. B. Cross)

2355 [FHA 859]
The deep-domed roof of the Brush body on 2355 is most noticeable as it stands in the forecourt of Stourbridge Town railway station. All the rebuilt F.E.D.D.s had rubber mounted saloon windows, as did this 1950 Hooton rebuild, but this did not detract too much from their original appearance. Both FHA series had the later prewar style of radiator which gave the vehicle a more modern look but somehow plagiarised A.E.C. radiator design. (A. B. Cross)

2359 [FHA 863]
The Midland "Red" operation in the Black Country was not generally hampered by low railway bridges and level crossings were fairly rare. However, in Station Road, Langley, the 122 route crossed the ex-G.W.R. Birmingham to Stourbridge line near Langley Green station. 2359 has just passed the Shell and B.P. oil storage yard and is about to cross the level crossing, which, today, is still in use but with lifting barriers.   (A. B. Cross)

2368 [FHA 872]
The driver of 2368 gets into his cab using the time-honoured Midland "Red" method of 'foot on the wheel rim, hand in cab and heave'. The bus is at the Bear Hotel. The F.E.D.D. is working the rather circuitous and popular 229 route to Blackheath, through Oldbury and Portway. It was a journey which entailed a number of very stiff climbs, especially around Portway which lies beneath the formidable Turners Hill, an igneous outcrop of Rowley Rag which rises to 876 ft. and forms part of the main watershed in England. The bus still has gold lining-out around the cab dash and body panels.   (A. B. Cross)

2405 [GHA 324] & 2406 [GHA 325]
The last prewar style S.O.S. vehicles delivered to Midland "Red" in 1940 were fifty Brush bodied thirty-eight seater S.O.N.s. After some ten years service, thirty seven of them had their bodies rebuilt by Nudd Bros. & Lockyer, which extended their lives by another seven or eight years, making them the last front-engined single-deckers new to Midland "Red" to stay in service. The rebuilding replaced the old half-drop windows with top sliders. The prewar mouldings were generally removed, although, in the case of 2405, a remnant below the cab and windscreen remained. 2406 is devoid of these embellishments. The two buses are parked in Burton bus station. (R. Marshall)

2428 [GHA 347] & 4002 [SHA 402]
The last S.O.N. types had Brush B38F bodies. They were usually garaged in the more distant parts of the Midland "Red" area and therefore to see one in service in the West Midlands was something of a rarity. 2428, with its pleasantly rounded body, stands in the market area of Birmingham with Leyland "Titan" PD2/12 4002. This area of Birmingham was redeveloped in the early 1960s when the Inner Ring Road was built. The S.O.S. was one of the last withdrawals of its class, going in 1958. One vehicle, 2418 [GHA 337], survives at the B.a.M.M.O.T. museum at Wythall. (S. N. J. White)

27

2432 [GHA 786]
In 1942, Midland "Red" were allocated some fifteen buses by the Ministry of War Transport. These were constructed from parts that were in stock at the manufacturers and 'frozen' from completion by the Government so that military vehicles could take precedence. 2432, the first of these buses, was a Leyland "Titan" TD7 with a Duple 'utility' body. In 1951, the body was rebuilt by Hooton. As a result, the rugged simple styling shown in the next picture, was lost beneath the caravan-style windows. The built-up cab front and nearside wing was intended to make the vehicle look more modern. 2432, seen parked in Wolverhampton on Railway Drive, was withdrawn in 1954.   (S. N. J. White)

2436 [GHA 790]
A Leyland "Titan" TD7 in original condition, 2436, with an angular Duple utility body, still retaining its stencil route number display, is in Navigation Street, Birmingham. It is about to work the long 196 route to Stafford via Wolverhampton. Leyland Motors had attempted, with this model, to produce a Diesel-engined chassis with the quiet running characteristics of a petrol engine. Despite the rather basic body, the chassis was, therefore, quite sophisticated, but the penalty for this smooth performance was a slow gear change due to the very large flywheel.   (D. R. Harvey collection)

28

2440 [GHA 794]
Northern Counties (N.C.M.E.) bodies were always something of a rarity in the West Midlands, as were Leyland "Titan" double-deckers, with only Birmingham City Transport having any quantity of the latter. In 1942 Midland "Red" acquired three vehicles which had the unusual combination of N.C.M.E. bodies and Leyland "Titan" TD7 chassis. The last one of these was 2440, which stands in Paradise Street, Birmingham, before resuming its duty on the 126 route to Wolverhampton, a service associated with these buses. Between 2440 and the unidentified silver-roofed F.E.D.D. stands the terracotta brick façade of Queens College Chambers, constructed in 1904 and which survives today as a frontage to a mid 1980s office complex. (S. N. J. White)

2441 [GHA 795]
It has never been made clear why Midland "Red" were allocated six A.E.C. "Regent" 0661s with Brush fifty-nine seat bodies in 1942. They were diverted from Coventry Corporation, when that municipality was crying out for buses after the 1940 blitz. The A.E.C. 7.7 litre Diesel engines were already used in the D.O.N. type single-deckers of 1934 and 1935, but it was a strange allocation of buses by the Ministry of War Transport. 2441 stands in Navigation Street in the early postwar days wearing a gold lined-out livery which also included two cream bands and a silver roof. These buses were all withdrawn about 1954 after arduous service in the Black Country. (R. A. Mills)

2500 [GHA 924]
Bus bodies which had been intended for Manchester Corporation became available to other operators about 1942. This was because of the Ministry of War Transport's 'unfrozen' policy where the intended chassis manufacturer totally diverted into building military vehicles or, as with Daimlers, the factory being destroyed by bomb damage. Midland "Red" received two bodies which were fitted to Guy "Arab" chassis. 2500, the second vehicle, is in High Street, Birmingham, on the 118 route to Walsall via Six Ways, Aston.   (R. A. Mills)

2512 [GHA 936] & 3504 [MHA 504]
New Street, Birmingham, was always one of the main termini for Midland "Red" services to the north and east of the city. In May 1956, buses for Water Orton, Sutton and Walsall, load up outside King Edward House. This was built in the 1930s on the site of the medieval King Edward's School. The leading vehicle is 2512, a 1943 Daimler CWA6 with a Weymann body which, despite its rebuild by Willowbrook in 1951, was beginning to show signs of advanced body deterioration. It was in its last few months of operation. The second bus is 3504, a 1950 Brush bodied B.M.M.O. D5, which had only a thirteen year service life with the company.   (G. H. F. Atkins)

30

2537 [GHA 972]
Midland "Red" received some thirty three Daimler CWA6 buses from the Ministry of War Transport's allocations and the body contracts were split between Brush, Weymann and, in the case of 2537, Duple. The latter's products were generally regarded as being among the better of the composite framed 'utility' bodies, but, in common with all Midland "Red"s utilities, was extensively rebuilt. GHA 945 is in its final unrebuilt state in lined out all-over red livery with a silver roof. It waits in Walsall bus station on 13/3/1950 before returning to Birmingham. (J. Cull)

2541 [HHA 1]
The penultimate S.O.S. chassis belied the extraordinary wartime product which served as a prototype for Midland "Red" postwar double-decker production. 2541 was the B.M.M.O. D1 built in late 1944. Its chassis was really a much modified F.E.D.D. unit but featured the refinement of servo-assisted brakes. The main difference from the prewar double-deckers lay in the body, which was a four-bay, metal-framed structure with a rear entrance layout built by Weymann. After wartime experiments with EHA 299, the D1 employed a trend-setting concealed radiator that was to influence other chassis manufacturers some five years later. It is seen at the Scott Arms on Walsall Road on the 119 route quite late in its twenty one year career. Interestingly, no further body contracts were ever again awarded to Weymanns. (A. B. Cross)

2549 [GHA 999]
The wartime Daimlers of Midland "Red" were allocated to the Birmingham garages as their preselector gearboxes were best suited to the busy conditions found on these often high frequency urban routes. 2549, the last CWA6 to be delivered, with a rebuilt Brush fifty-six seat body, stands outside Acocks Green library in the early 1950s. A number of services started from this southeastern suburb. This bus, however, displays the route number 155, which went from the Bull Ring along the A41 to Solihull and then beyond to the village of Knowle. Acocks Green is still linked today to Solihull by various bus services, including some operated by minibuses. (S. N. J. White)

2561 [HHA 13]
The uncompromisingly angular lines of the Weymann utility body on 2561, a 1944 Guy "Arab" II, almost suggest the quality of ride afforded by the Gardner 5LW engined buses. Originally fitted with wooden slatted seats, at least the upholstered replacements absorbed a little of the vibrations caused by the unflexibly mounted engine. Most of the Birmingham area's wartime Guys were allocated to Sutton garage. 2561 is seen in Walsall bus station about 1950. Their drivers must have been glad to have seen them withdrawn by 1955, thus ensuring that they would no longer have to struggle with the Guy's reverse-gated crash gearboxes.   (R. A. Mills)

2579 [HHA 222]
The contrast between 2579 and the unidentified Bedford OWB with a Duple utility body, built only two or three years earlier, could hardly be greater. The B.M.M.O. single-decker was the final preproduction underfloor-engined prototype and was classified S5. Although superficially resembling the S6 to S13 series, this M.C.C.W. bodied bus was of chassisless design as were the later S14 vehicles of 1954. The only clue to this was the wide pillar behind the driver's door, designed to give the structure more rigidity. It is seen in Station Street, Birmingham, in early postwar years, with the war-damaged roof of New Street station behind.
(W. J. Haynes)

2584 [HHA 61]
Parked in Hinckley Street, at the rear of Birmingham's Repertory Theatre, are Guy "Arab" IIs 2584 and 2585. Both vehicles had been extensively rebuilt by Brush in 1951, effectively hiding the angular lines of the Park Royal utility bodies. Unfortunately, the intensive use given to these buses, especially in the Birmingham area, exposed the frailties of the wartime wooden body framing. In common with all of the Midland "Red"s 106 Ministry of Supply allocated double-deckers, 2584 and 2585 were both withdrawn in 1955, a mere four years after their rebuilding. (S. N. J. White)

DIGBETH
Digbeth was the centre of Midland "Red" operation in the Birmingham area. In the early postwar years buses allocated to the garage had to be parked on land between the covered accommodation and the main thoroughfare. This view taken across Digbeth from the southeast can be dated fairly precisely. Neither the FHA registered F.E.D.D. nor the Duple bodied Daimler CWA6 double-deckers have had their bodies rebuilt and the Brush bodied B.M.M.O. S6, parked behind the O.N.C. coach, was delivered in 1947. This, coupled with the trolleybus and tram wires still being in situ, suggests a date of about 1948.

(Courtesy West Midlands Travel)

3000 [HHA 601]
The B.M.M.O. S6 underfloor single-decker was years ahead of other manufacturers' products when it entered service in 1946. The Company management realised that such a trend-setting vehicle should have a significant fleet number. The original number 2601 was not used, but the prebooked registration numbers were, accounting for the apparently out-of-step registration HHA 601. It is seen at Barnsley Hall Hospital on the 328 route in July 1964. This vehicle lasted until later the same year when pleas were made to Midland "Red" to preserve it. Unfortunately, Mr. D. M. Sinclair would have none of this, saying that "the perfect bus has not been built", inferring that this revolutionary vehicle was not worth saving. (A. A. Turner)

3002 [HHA 603]
Towards the end of their careers, the S6s, perhaps more than the later B.M.M.O. type single-deckers, began to look decidedly dated and run down. Whether this was because they were narrower, at 7ft. 6in., or that their somewhat 'dejected' frontal appearance gave this impression, it is difficult to say; certainly, it would seem that 3002 had seen better days. It is parked outside Oldbury garage next to the 'art deco' style company office, both of which opened in April 1937. The bodies order on the S6 batch of one hundred buses was split between Brush and M.C.C.W. This is one of the products of one of the former body builder. Oldbury garage was usually associated with double-decker operation; it had, at various times, most types of single-decker, but the S6 was something of a rarity. (A. D. Broughall)

35

3011 [HHA 612]
The road from Bridgnorth to Stourbridge via Enville and Kinver is a rather tortuous one, being narrow, twisting and interspersed with short climbs and steep descents. 3011, a 1947 vintage B.M.M.O. S6 with a M.C.C.W. body, has just made the ascent from the Severn Valley at Bridgnorth with a good load of passengers. All the early postwar saloons were built to 27ft. 6in. length, but were extended to 29ft. 3in. thereby increasing their seating capacity by four to B44F. This work was carried out by Charles Roe in 1953 and involved extending the rear overhang. The rear side window became much longer as a result of the rebuilding. The classic 'big Bedford' SB with the first style of Duple body visible in the side road is working on Foxall's service from the now long closed Stanmore R.A.F. camp. (A. B. Cross)

3046 [HHA 647]
Dr. Samuel Johnson, lexicographer, philosopher and man of letters, sits deep in thought above rebuilt B.M.M.O. S6 3046. The bus waits in Johnson's home city of Lichfield before beginning the run on the 765 route to Tamworth, Atherstone and Nuneaton before completing its journey in Coventry. The horizontal version of the eight litre 'K' engine was used in these single-deckers. This was coupled to a David Brown constant-mesh gearbox and with the bonus of a well insulated interior, made for a fairly speedy and comfortable ride. In fact, early in their careers the S6s were used to augment the prewar coach fleet until the delivery of the C1 vehicles in 1950. (R. Wilson)

3071 [HHA 672] & 3584 [NHA 584]
The difference in width between the S6, 3071, and the 8ft. wide S10, 3584 behind, is noticeable as they both descend Regent Street, Leamington Spa, whilst working town services. The S6 class had the body contract split between M.C.C.W. and Brush, an example of the latter being 3071, which weighed about 3 cwt. more than the M.C.C.W. buses at 6 tons 16 cwts. There were superficial differences with the Brush bodies having squarer destination boxes and slightly lower side lights which gave a 'thinner appearance' at the front. The buildings in Regent Street are more diverse in style, lacking the architectural unity of some of Leamington's grander residential areas.   (A. B. Cross)

3100/3106/3107 [JHA 1/7/8]
Twelve brand new, sparklingly-painted A.E.C. "Regent" II 0661s with Brush H30/26R bodies have been lined up in echelon in 1948. Their destination boxes have been wound on to show the terminal points of the 130 route Stourbridge via Halesowen, which these buses worked for a number of years. The A.E.C. "Regent" II's normal appearance had been drastically altered by the D1 style enclosed bonnet, yet these AD2 class buses were hardly any advance on the 'unfrozen' Coventry style "Regents" of 1942. In this view, the top of the windscreen is level with the bottom of the canopy, but such was the driving position that the windscreen was later raised some three inches to improve the driver's view.   (B.M.M.O.; R. Marshall collection)

37

3118 [JHA 19] & 3560 [MHA 60]
The wide Market Place in Dudley was created in the early 1860s after the old Town Hall had been demolished. The Dudley fountain, an elaborately embellished structure, was opened by the Countess of Dudley on 17 October 1867, wishing it 'a career of usefulness'. Having survived being regarded as a Victorian monstrosity and a traffic hazard, it is now a focal point of the Market Place which is today a pedestrianised precinct. The early 19th century buildings behind the A.E.C. "Regent" II, 3118, were obliterated in the 1960s rebuilding of part of the town centre. The A.E.C. and Guy "Arab" III, 3560, are both working the Stourbridge 246 route.   (R. Wilson)

3138 [JHA 39]
Brush bodied A.E.C. "Regent" II, 3138, stands in High Street, Solihull. It is working the 154 route, a service which went along the busy Stratford Road via Shirley. The High Street in Solihull in the early 1950s still displayed the characteristics of a large medieval and Georgian village rather medium sized town. Even today, behind the façades of multinational retailers with their monotonous 'in-house' frontages, much of old Solihull remains. 3138 is still in the lined-out style of livery and has yet to receive ventilators in the front dome.   (R. Wilson)

3162 [JHA 63]
Some rural services hardly seemed to merit the use of double-deckers. By the end of the 1950s the availability of private cars had dramatically reduced the numbers of passengers using public transport. Midland "Red" suffered as badly as any operator in this respect, although 3162 does not seem to have much competition, judging by the deserted road. This A.E.C. "Regent" II carries an M.C.C.W. H30/26R body. It is working the 554 route from Bishops Itchington to the Lockheed Works, an extension of the route beyond Leamington town centre. 3162 is passing through that part of southern Warwickshire known for its abandoned medieval villages, on 22/10/1962. (D. R. Harvey collection)

3183 [JHA 84]
The AD2 class of A.E.C. "Regent" IIs had the A.E.C. 7.7 litre Diesel engines. It was soon realised that they were underpowered, particularly as their weight with M.C.C.W. bodies of 7 tons 10 cwt. left them struggling for performance on hilly routes. 3183 is one of the fifty of the class bodied by M.C.C.W. It had been transferred early in its career to Stafford garage whose operating area had a gentle terrain, and it is seen here on 30/8/1960 working the S89 route via Kingston Hill. Metro-Cammell, who were, at the time, concentrating on building bus bodies for London Transport and Birmingham City Transport, were very late in delivering these vehicles as they were a one-off design. 3183 entered service in 1950 and was one of the first withdrawals in 1961. (G. Pattison)

39

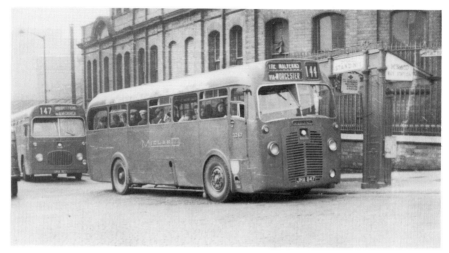

3247 [JHA 847] & 4327 [UHA 327]
The old British Railways parcels office at the top of Station Street, Birmingham, had seen better days. It is March 1957 and this part of Birmingham's city centre had never recovered from the wartime attentions of the Luftwaffe. B.M.M.O. 3247, a S8 with an extended M.C.C.W. B44F body, still carries the early style of shaded fleet numerals. It is well laden for the journey to Worcester and the Malverns. Behind it is the almost new B.M.M.O. S14, 4327, which had entered service, along with six others of the class, with the normal arrangement of twin pairs of rear wheels. As can be seen, it had soon reverted to the unusual, but standard, single rears. It is working the 147 route to Redditch via Alvechurch. (A. Richardson)

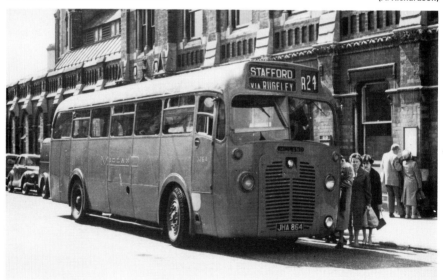

3264 [JHA 864]
Service 824 was typical of many Midland "Red" routes, serving two towns but deviating from the main road route so that, in this case, it could pass through the villages of Upper Longden and Colwich. The latter village has a very low bridge which has always necessitated using single-deck vehicles. In the late 1950s, 3264, a 1948 B.M.M.O. S8 with a lengthened M.C.C.W. B44F body, was considered appropriate for this duty. Hardly a lightweight vehicle at 6 tons 13 cwt., this particular bus lasted until 1963 before withdrawal. It is, however, beyond the first 'flush of youth' and has lost most of its chromework when it had been spray painted during its last overhaul. (A. B. Cross)

40

3308 [KHA 308]
The B.M.M.O. C1 class, built in 1948 and 1949, comprised forty five coaches whose Duple C30C bodies bore a family resemblance to the pre-war O.N.C. vehicles of 1939. Unlike them, however, the C1s were underfloor engined and were modified S6 chassis fitted with overdrive gearboxes. The bodies, despite a rather Americanised radiator grill, had a purposefulness and certainty of design which were lacking in other underfloor coach bodies for many years. 3308 is on the forecourt parking of Digbeth depot in 1952, with three F.E.D.D.s and B.M.M.O. D5B 3827. (S. N. J. White)

3356 [KHA 356]
The descent from the Scottish Highlands into Digbeth via Birmingham's Bull Ring on a damp, dreary day, might have been an anticlimax after a week's touring. Midland "Red" tours to Scotland, the Lake District and Devon and Cornwall, were very well patronised, being regarded as something slightly superior to other coach tours. 3356 was nine years old when it was rebuilt in 1959 to modernise its appearance. With their overdrive gearbox and stylish coachwork by Duple which actually "got it right" in design terms, these solidly built vehicles bore the bulk of such touring for an extraordinarily long time; in this case 3356 was withdrawn in 1966. (A. B. Cross)

41

3390 [LHA 393]
Bridgnorth had three town services, the B90, B91 and the school service B92. A Wellington allocated B.M.M.O. S9, 3393, with a Brush B44F body built in 1949, climbs through Bridgnorth on this short service. It is also noticeable that on none of the vehicles operated by Midland "Red" until the late 1950s was provision made for direction indicators. It was hand signals or frequently nothing! (A. B. Cross)

3403 [LHA 403] & 3988 [SHA 388]
3403, a 1949 Brush bodied S9, is standing in Dudley Bus station while working the D1 route to the Priory Estate, a municipal housing estate, begun in 1926, which for many years, supplied Midland "Red" with a lot of revenue. Behind it, a few concrete shelters away is 3988, one of the hundred all-Leyland "Titan" PD2/12s ordered in 1953, which is working on the 281 route via Woodcross to Wolverhampton. The steep slope of Birmingham Street, Dudley, was a less than satisfactory place to site a bus station but despite a few incidents of buses rolling away, it served the town for many years. (A. B. Cross)

3404 [LHA 404]
There were no medieval houses in Northgate left after the "Great Fire of Warwick" in 1694, although the parish church St. Mary's, which stands majestically on the high ground between the Market Place and East Gate, survived. It and the rest of the town were gradually rebuilt in the eighteenth century, with the result that Warwick has one of the finest, yet surely least recognised, Georgian town centres. 3404, one of the 3357-3456 class of B.M.M.O. S9s comes down Northgate Street before turning left into Jury Street and then on to Leamington.
(A. B. Cross)

3471 [MHA 471]
The B.M.M.O. D5 series of one hundred Brush bodied double-deckers was a development of the prototype D1, but were eight feet wide. They were splendidly robust-looking buses, yet withdrawals began in 1962 and all were gone four years later. 3471, built in 1949, survived some sixteen years. It is seen towards the end of its operational life, almost full to capacity, tackling the hill up to the Wolverhampton Road on the 229 route after leaving Oldbury. The driver has his left hand around the gearlever and will do a double-declutch change down the gearbox.
(A. D. Broughall)

3501 [MHA 501]
3501, a 1949 D5, has just left Broad Street, having passed Baskerville House, visible on the extreme left, and is travelling along the short length of Easy Row, before turning into Paradise Street. It is working the 122 service from Oldbury about 1962. Easy Row lay where the present Central Reference Library is today. In that complex is Fletcher's Walk, named after the landlord for many years of the "Woodman", probably Birmingham's finest Victorian public house. The "Woodman" is masked by 3501 and like the bus, also disappeared in the 1960's.
(R. H. G. Simpson)

3516 [MHA 516]
Resplendent in its gold lined-out red livery with black mud wings, 3516 calls at Rose Bank Gardens, Malvern, before journeying to Birmingham. The B.M.M.O. D5 class were bodied by Brush of Loughborough who had constructed Midland "Red" bodies since the 1920s and continued to do so until they closed in 1952. The D5s featured one of the neater concealed radiator designs, spoilt, perhaps, by the rather fussy central grill. With a 7¾ ton body powered by the B.M.M.O. 'K' type engine, any journey on a hilly route, such as the 144, with a full load would have been stately rather than spritely.
(S. N. J. White)

3522 [MHA 522]
A 1935 Austin "Ruby" Seven bounces over the cobbles in Station Street, Birmingham, descending past the Hercules Cycle advertisement, towards the Market Hotel. The site of that hoarding and everything on the incline was redeveloped into the Bull Ring Shopping Centre and the bus station complex which was opened in November 1963. The D5, 3522, carries the Crawfords Cream Cracker advertisement which was painted onto the between-deck panels and were such a livery-enhancing feature of the mid 1950s Midland "Red" double-deckers. It is on the 144 route and is parked in front of the later M.C.C.W. bodied B.M.M.O. D7.   (A. B. Cross)

3553 [MHA 553]
The B.M.M.O. D5s had substantial Brush built bodies and were well known for their reliability and quiet performance. The offside front tyre of 3553 looks well worn as it stands in the old Oldbury bus station. This was swept away in the 1980s when the Savacentre hypermarket was built. Whereas municipal operators were getting nearly twenty years service out of their vehicles, Midland "Red" only got thirteen out of this particular bus. It was withdrawn in 1963, but had run very intensively from Oldbury garage for much of its life on the heavily subscribed Black Country services.   (A. D. Broughall)

3567 [MHA 67]
The twenty Guy "Arab" IIIs of the GD6 class (3557-3576) were always associated with Dudley garage and therefore to see one away from its usual haunts is most unusual. 3567, on the 118 route to Walsall, crosses the Queslett Road traffic lights on Walsall Road at the Scott Arms. The hanging lantern light visible on the extreme right belonged to the Scott Arms pub, which was built in the 1870s as a coaching inn. This historic building, demolished in May 1966 because of the impending road widening, marks the Birmingham boundary and gives its name to this part of Great Barr. Two B.M.M.O. D7 double-deckers are at the Birmingham to Great Barr 119 route terminus.
(A. B. Cross)

3570 [MHA 70]
With its narrow, almost prewar F.E.D.D. width cab, 3570, a Guy "Arab" III with a Guy H30/26R body built on Park Royal frames, storms up Long Lane towards Quinton. It is working the 140 route from Dudley to Birmingham, a service for which these powerful buses were eminently suited. The vehicles, with their Meadows 6DC engines, were bought in 1949 because of a chronic shortage of new double-deckers. The large engines were awkward to maintain as all the auxiliaries, such as injectors and fuel system, were on the cabside of the engine. They were re-engined in 1952 with the more sedentary B.M.M.O. K unit and their fabulous hill-climbing performances around the Black Country were never recaptured.
(A. B. Cross)

3571 [MHA 71]
The Wulfrunian combination of Guy built bodies and Meadows engines allowed for top gear running on all but the steepest hills. 3571 is in Blackheath after working the short, but demanding 232 route from Old Hill. The direct route between the two towns was via the very steep Waterfall Lane. The Birmingham and Midland Tramway Company built the much less steep, but longer, Perry Park Road which was subsequently used by Midland "Red" 232 route. This bus, fitted with a rather basic Park Royal framed Guy body, was also structurally rebuilt at Carlyle Road works during the 1950s, but, despite this, was withdrawn as early as 1962 and sent for scrap when only thirteen years old.   (A. B. Cross)

3616 [NHA 616]
The 293 route started from the delightfully named Far Forest and ran to Kidderminster via Bewdley, in whose splendid Georgian High Street 3616 is standing. This is a B.M.M.O. S10 with a Brush B44F body built in 1950 and extended by C. Roe of Crossgates, Leeds, in 1952 from its original B40F configuration. Bewdley, with its magnificent Telford designed bridge over the River Severn, might have grown larger if it had accepted the offer of the canal being built from Stourbridge to link up with the river. The town refused the offer and England's only canal 'new town' was built at Stourport, a few miles down stream.   (A. B. Cross)

3670 [NHA 670]
The newly lengthened 3670 stands at Bartley Green, after working the 208 route from Birmingham via the Howley Grange Estate and Woodgate. The area, part in Birmingham part in Halesowen, lies on the fringe of the West Midlands conurbation and was developed as an overspill for Birmingham. This Brush bodied S10 was built in 1950 and was one of the first withdrawn in 1963. These were the last type of Midland "Red" single-deckers to be built to 27ft. 6in. in length, but were first to have all the main bays with ventilator windows. They also were the first B.M.M.O. postwar single-deckers to have the handbrake in the orthodox position on the offside of the cab.
(A. B. Cross)

3676 [NHA 676]
1950 B.M.M.O. Brush bodied S10 3676 leaves Hereford bus station on the H2 route. The bus station is next to the 1930s Odeon-style cinema. Midland "Red", for many years the main operator in the city, ran some fourteen city services in Hereford. 3676 leaves the bus station to take up service on the H2 route to Westfields.
(G. Pattison)

3700 [NHA 700]
Sandwiched between the prototype S13, 3694, and the only S11 was a small batch of eight B.M.M.O. S10s. 3700, one of four bodied by M.C.C.W., turns off the A442, just south of the unusually named hamlet of Quatt. It is going to the small mining village of Alveley on the 297 route from Bridgnorth to Kidderminster. The Vauxhall Victor's unrusted bodywork would date this view about the early 1960s. (R. F. Mack)

3712 [NHA 712]
An unrebuilt B.M.M.O. S10, with a Brush body, stands in Queens Drive, Birmingham, in 1951 when one year old. It operated for two years in this condition before being extended by C. Roe to increase its seating capacity by four to B44F. This was made possible on all the early postwar S type single-deckers as they did have rather long wheelbases and short rear overhangs in their original form. 3712 [NHA 712] waits in front of 3409 [LHA 409], a 1949 B.M.M.O. S9, which would also be lengthened in 1952. (S. N. J. White)

49

3784 [NHA 784]
The early postwar Standard four-door saloon seems something of an anachronism in comparison with the Austin "Mini" Seven, as they stand in Hereford city centre outside the Cafe Marguerite and surrounded by Georgian and Victorian buildings. This early 1960s scene marks an historical transitional period; long term redevelopment had not really begun, and shops often had a run down look, having been unaltered since before the war. 3784, a 1951 B.M.M.O. D5B, was not withdrawn until 1965. Yet the contrasts between old and new cars, uncared for buildings and perhaps outmoded buses is typical of the period. (G. Pattison)

3786 [NHA 786]
The innovation of platform doors on the 1950 to 1952 deliveries of Brush bodied B.M.M.O. DB5s must have been most welcome in periods of inclement weather. The 159 service ran between Birmingham and Coventry. 3786 is parked in Spiceal Street, with the Bull Ring bus shelters belonging to Midland "Red" visible to the right of the bus. The C.W.S. advertisement was more commonly found on the buses and trams of the Birmingham municipal fleet in the 1952 to 1954 period than on Midland "Red" vehicles. 3786 is in what is now a narrow pedestrianised street and the buildings in the background and the tram traction pole are just a memory. (S. N. J. White)

50

3791 [NHA 791]
Waiting at Railway Drive, Wolverhampton, to go on the long 885 route to Kidderminster via Stourbridge is 3791. The Brush H30/26R bodied B.M.M.O. D5B has fairly recently been spray painted and, as a consequence, has lost its gold lining-out and black wings. By economising on the painted appearance of their buses, Midland "Red" certainly lived up to their name, but this produced somehow more drab looking vehicles. It was, in this case, the sensational corner panel advertisements in the *Empire News* that brightened up the appearance of this vehicle.
(S. N. J. White)

3813 [NHA 813]
The D5B is leaving Bearwood on the 221 route to West Bromwich, but no one in the bus station appears to have reminded either the driver or conductor to wind back the destination blind on 3813. The bus is in Lightwoods Hill, near Warley Woods, on an autumnal day in the autumn of the bus' career. The somewhat 'worried' frontal aspect of these heavyweight double-deckers is well shown as it approaches the top of the long climb from Bearwood.
(A. D. Broughall)

3821 [NHA 821]
3821 stands empty in an equally deserted Stourbridge Town station yard on 21/8/1961. The bus station is opposite the bus garage, which unusually, served as an undercover starting point for a number of services. For many years Stourbridge's buses were mainly single-deckers because of the very low Foster Street railway bridge just a few yards away from the garage. Brand new AD2s were allocated for the conversion of the 130 route, and, when it was discovered that they were underpowered, B.M.M.O. D5s and D5Bs became the normal allocation for the garage. This D5B was withdrawn in 1964. (R. F. Mack)

3839 [NHA 839]
Tamworth is on a bridging point of the River Tame and stands on a series of low terraces above the wide valley. The bus station in which 3839, a 1951 B.M.M.O. D5B is parked, was adjacent to the bus garage some distance away from the river. It is working the 198 route to Birmingham and would cross the wide, flat Tame valley on its way to the city via Drayton Manor, later to develop into one of the larger leisure parks in the Midlands. Midland "Red" used a most pungent cleaning fluid, whose odour, like that of tar, was irresistible yet quite revolting. On hot days, such as this one, long periods of exposure to it were nauseating. The combination of the heat and the smell led to the desire for extra ventilation. (D. R. Harvey collection)

3913 [OHA 913]
The B.M.M.O. S13 were the last of the underfloor engined S-type single-deckers to be built with a separate chassis and body. There were ninety-nine vehicles, including four prototypes. The main production series were numbered 3880-3975. Some were bodied by Nudd Bros. & Lockyer and some by Brush. The production S13s were built as dual purpose vehicles and as such were occasionally required to cover long journeys when coaches were not available. 3913, a Nudd Bros. bodied example, is at Victoria coach station in London, waiting to return to Coventry, when about two years old. (A. B. Cross)

3941 [OHA 941]
The redevelopment of Birmingham in the 1960s meant that often temporary roads were built across what looked like a demolition site. One such road between Moor Street and the Bull Ring was built behind the Marks and Spencer store. A glorified turning circle served as a temporary bus terminus, between the closure of the area in front of St. Martin's in the Bull Ring, and the opening in 1964 of the Bull Ring bus station. 3941, a B.M.M.O. S13 with a Brush DP40F body works on the 176 probably on a shortworking as the route went to Solihull via Sheldon. (A. D. Broughall)

3951 [OHA 951]
Dual purpose B.M.M.O. S13s were repainted in the black and red coach livery in 1956 and, although the dual purpose S15 was introduced the following year, these solidly built single-deckers were used during the next eight years for express service alongside the newer, lighter and faster vehicles. 3951, a Nudd Bros. & Lockyer bodied example with a DP40F seating layout, is in Dudley bus station on 21/5/1961, working the more menial 262 service between Dudley and Bilston. Just visible in the background is 4944 [1944 HA], the second B.M.M.O. D10, which is at the site of the present Dudley bus station.
(G. Pattison)

4020 [SHA 420]
Midland "Red" had used the area in front of St. Martin's Church in Birmingham's Bull Ring since their early days of operation. Midland "Red" crews had spent their lay over time at the wooden tea bar, near to the corrugated iron bus shelters, before embarking on journeys to Warwick, Stratford or perhaps, as in this case, Coventry. 4020 an almost new LD8 type is an all-Leyland vehicle and is working the 159 route via Stonebridge and Meriden via the A45. These Leyland 0.600 9.8 litre powered buses were best suited to these longer routes and recorded very high mileages in somewhat short careers. This bus was taken out of service in 1966 when only thirteen years old.
(A. B. Cross)

54

4025 [SHA 425]
A rather dusty 4025 travels through the Victorian suburb of Sparkbrook, Birmingham, while working the twenty three mile long 150 route, also worked by Stratford Blue Motors. These Midland "Red" vehicles had the 'Faringdon' style of round cornered window pans that characterised the last few years of Leyland double-deck bodywork design. The 3978-4077 class was built with a front end design specified by Midland "Red". They were the only Leyland bodied buses to have this front from new, although Edinburgh Corporation rebuilt some 1952 exposed radiator examples and the pre-production design mock-up was built on the Leyland "Titan" demonstrator, NTF 9.
(S. N. J. White)

4040 [SHA 440]
Despite the loss of its gold lining-out, 4040 still looks extremely smart as it stands on the cobbles on the wrong side of Worcester Street, Birmingham. Behind are the Doric columns of the Market Hall which was severely bomb-damaged in August 1940. These Leyland "Titans" have always had a confused classification. Strictly speaking, they are PD2/12s, i.e. synchromesh gearbox and vacuum brakes, fitted with enclosed radiators. It was only after their completion that Leyland Motors classified all concealed radiator PD2/12s as PD2/20s. Therefore all further references to these vehicles are as PD2/12s.
(S. N. J. White)

4056 [SHA 456]
4056, a 1953 Leyland bodied PD2/12, is in Pool Meadow bus station, Coventry, which for many years, displayed an air of a temporary terminus whose very transience encouraged the feeling of unkempt decay. 4056 is working the 517 route back to its home town via Kenilworth. The Leamington allocation of these LD8 vehicles led a particularly hard life, as they were used on services to Coventry and the Leamington town routes. The bus has been spray painted and has a relocated registration plate. Behind it is 4346 [UHA 346], a 1956 B.M.M.O. S14, which is working on the 538 route to Kenilworth.
(R. Marshall)

4062 [SHA 462]
Midland "Red" did not operate many services totally within the Birmingham boundary, but certain routes did terminate in the city's suburbs. The short 201 route started in Smethwick and meandered its way via Warley across the main Hagley Road West (the A456) to finish by the small row of shops at Faraday Avenue, Quinton. 4062 is at this terminus in the twilight of its career in 1965, and is one of Bearwood garage's allocation of these vehicles. It is surprising, in view of the somewhat wallowing ride which characterised these vehicles, that they were rostered for such a tortuous urban route.
(M. Collignon)

4081 [THA 81]
Between 1953 and 1957 B.M.M.O. built some three hundred and fifty D7 type double-deckers which were all bodied by M.C.C.W. The lightweight bodies were much plainer than those on the D5 and D5B buses and had visual echoes of the "Orion" types. The result was a 7 ton 7 cwt. sixty-three seater (although the first ones originally sat only fifty-eight). They were distributed throughout the Midland "Red" operating area for use mainly on urban routes such as those serving Leicester, Birmingham and the Black Country. 4081, the third built D7, is in Market Street, Kidderminster town centre, on 16/5/1961. (R. F. Mack)

4091 [THA 91] & 5394 [AHA 394B]
The lower destination blind on 4091 is not so much lazy as terminally damaged; it should read "Red Hill". Double-deck operation only came to Hereford in 1950 and was invaluable on the X34 and X35 services which ran to Shrewsbury via Leominster, Ludlow and Church Stretton along the A49. This road roughly marked the western boundary of Midland "Red" operations. 4091 was one of the D7s allocated for this and Hereford's city services and is seen at St. Peter's Church, along with one of the B.M.M.O. D9s, 5394 [AHA 394B], which eventually replaced the D7 class. (A. B. Cross)

4093 [THA 93]
Worcester's main bus station for country services was Newport Street, which lay between the River Severn and the nearby city centre streets, which were used for local services. In the late 1950s, D7 4093 is working the 144 route and is fairly full as it prepares to pull away for the journey to Malvern. The D7s were the first Midland "Red" class to have the new more robust B.M.M.O. KL (Kidney Long) type of engine. The D7, with its quiet but nonetheless crash gearbox, was very much a drivers' bus and the long run from Birmingham would have been much more of a "slog" than in the faster LD8s. (S. N. J. White)

4114 [THA 114]
The last B.M.M.O. D7 to remain in P.S.V. service was 4114 which was not withdrawn until 1973. It was allocated to Dudley garage and is shown carrying the then latest style of Midland "Red" fleet name. It is passing Upland Road between Blackheath and Dudley when working the 141 route. The D7s were associated with many of the more heavily subscribed Black Country services which operated over very indifferent road surfaces caused by mining subsidence. As a result, the M.C.C.W. lightweight bodies rattled about and it is, therefore, surprising that it was a Dudley allocated D7 which was the last to be withdrawn. (A. D. Broughall)

58

4185 [UHA 185]
The Midland "Red" company was justifiably proud of both its long distance express coach work and the 'cruising' trips which, for so long, featured prominently in its advertising. 4185, a 1954 B.M.M.O. C3 coach was one of sixty three somewhat over-curvaceously styled Willowbrook C37C bodied C3s. It stands in Cleveland Road, Wolverhampton, having its boot loaded with luggage. These coaches epitomised the Midland "Red" style for their twelve year service lives and, although seventeen were rebodied by Plaxton, they never quite captured the flair of the vehicles when in their original form. (S. N. J. White)

4249 [UHA 249]
B.M.M.O. C4, 4249, leaves the Black and White coach station at Cheltenham Spa. These touring coaches were a modified version of the C3 class, having four curved glass cant rail windows and only thirty-two seats. At 7 tons 7 cwt., they weighed about the same as the contemporary D7. The eleven C4s were bodied by W. Alexander and it is interesting that this bodybuilder was willing to build such a 'one-off' order that was so different in style from its normal products. Cheltenham was used for passenger transfers by the Associated Motorways coaching pool as well as a refreshment stops on long journeys. (G. Pattison)

4271 [UHA 271]
The Wolverhampton to Ironbridge 892 route was operated by single-deckers because of height restrictions. By the late 1960s, S14 single-deckers were in use. 4271, one of 219 of this type of thirty foot long buses, enters Ironbridge. The town grew up because, in 1779, Abraham Darby built the world's first iron bridge which spans the River Severn. The town is, therefore, a delightful mixture of late Georgian, Regency and Victorian buildings each marking distinct periods of growth. Today it is the centre of Telford's "Cradle of the Industrial Revolution" museums. Ironbridge, it will be noticed, despite its small size, does have its own version of "Woolleys"!
(A. B. Cross)

4337 [UHA 337]
Route 252 was jointly operated with West Bromwich Corporation. It started on the Birmingham-Smethwick boundary at the B.C.T. No. 7 route terminus and went, via Roebuck Lane, to West Bromwich and Carters Green. 4337, a B.M.M.O. S14, stands in Carters Green, and is followed by West Bromwich Corporation 143 [DEA 543], a Daimler CVG6 with an unusual style of M.C.C.W. body. The 252 route might have been numbered 222, but in the days of stencils, no bus carries three number stencils the same. So there could be no routes numbered 111, 222, 333, etc. until roller blinds were universally available.
(A. D. Broughall)

60

4359 [VHA 359]
The D7s were, for many years, the real work horses of the Midland "Red" fleet. Although criticised for their rather parsimonious interior finish, they were mechanically very dependable and could be relied upon for either town services or long inter-urban routes. One of the second batch, 4359, is working from Stafford towards Walsall and Dudley on the 865 route. It is beneath Walsall Corporation trolleybus wires at the Bloxwich terminus, and is parked in front of one of that municipality's semi-low height Daimler CVG6s with a Willowbrook body, 840 [WDH 915]. (R. F. Mack)

4368 [VHA 368]
Although outwardly a standard D7, 4368 early in its career had been fitted with a two pedal control gearbox. Despite making the driver's life easier, the device was not a success. The bus is working the 252 route in Roebuck Lane, Smethwick, and is negotiating the narrow bridge over James Brindley's Birmingham canal, which was built in November 1769. Nearby is Thomas Telford's much later canal, spanned by the magnificent Galton Bridge. Roebuck Lane is today only used as an access road to an industrial estate. (A. D. Broughall)

61

4384 [VHA 384]
B.M.M.O. D7, 4384 ambles past the exit door of the then fairly recently reconstructed Stourbridge garage on 6/7/1961. Note the conductor on the top deck changing the destination blinds, hence the apparently misleading display. The bus is carrying an advertisement for the "Stourbridge Fireclay Mining Company", a reminder of the many brick making works in the area; most of these were to close by the early 1970s. The Odeon Cinema has long since shown its last film and Stourbridge garage was closed in January 1985.   (A. B. Cross)

4477 [XHA 477]
Carlyle Road Works produced some excellent double-deckers. The D5s and the D5Bs were stylish, quiet heavyweights, while the later D9 was an integral vehicle as advanced as its roughly contemporary thirty foot long A.E.C., "Routemaster". There were more D7s than any other of B.M.M.O.'s "home-produced" prewar or postwar double-deckers, yet these buses are given fairly scant praise for the sterling work that they did. 4477, a 1956 example, is seen in pristine condition in Cleveland Road, Wolverhampton, while on the 196 route from Stafford to Birmingham. Through passengers could only book as far as Wolverhampton and then had to pay again.   (S. N. J. White)

4489 [XHA 489]
4489, a 1956 B.M.M.O. D7, speeds through Lickey End on the 144 route to Malvern Wells in the late 1960s. This bus was among the later withdrawals, not being taken off the road until 1971. Lickey End is on the A38 between Rubery and Bromsgrove, but this fairly rural scene, with a chapel, a few Victorian houses and a small copse opposite, was lost for ever in the mid 1980s when construction began of the M42 motorway. The site of this photograph is now the middle of a large intersection with the motorway running some twenty feet below.
(A. D. Broughall)

4535 [XHA 535]
Wednesbury was only one of three towns in the West Midlands that the four municipal operators (Birmingham, Walsall, West Bromwich and Wolverhampton) and Midland "Red" actually served. 4535, a Dudley-garaged B.M.M.O. D7, is in Wednesbury bus station working the 244 route to Cradley Heath, a service which crossed the Black Country from the traditionally glass-blowing industrial area of the southwest to the heavy industry and mining region of the northeast.
(A. D. Broughall)

4561 [561 AHA]
The B.M.M.O. S14 were very advanced chassisless buses with disc-brakes on all wheels and rubber-mounted suspension. The buses had glassfibre sidepanels, one-piece moulded roofs and single rear wheels. The S14 class had the horizontal KL engine and yet, for a 30ft. single-decker, weighed only about 5¾ tons. 4561 belonged to the second batch, was built in 1957 and ran until 1970. It is seen in Worcester, approaching Newport Street bus station on the 417 route from Hereford via Ledbury. It is being followed by 5111 [5111 HA], a 1962 36ft long B.M.M.O. S16.
(A. D. Broughall)

4602 [602 AHA]
The S14 buses were ideal as ordinary service vehicles but lacked the refinement and comfort necessary for longer journeys. The B.M.M.O. S15 buses were the dual purpose development of the S14s and were designed for use on the longer stage carriage services. 4602, when nearly new and still fitted with the silver external transfers, is working the X96 route from Northampton to Shrewsbury via Birmingham. This was at one time the longest stage carriage route in England. 4602, the second of the class, is in Coventry's Pool Meadow bus station when quite new, with B.M.M.O. D7 4499 [XHA 499].
(A. B. Cross)

4621 [621 AHA]
The S15 dual purpose single-deckers were built in two batches: 4601-4650 in 1957 and 5045-5092 were completed to almost identical specifications some five years later. The latter were Midland "Red"'s last 30ft. long single-deckers. After three years, the earlier vehicles were downgraded to service buses. This usually entailed a repaint in all-over red and the fitting driver-issued ticket equipment. 4621 is in this condition and is in Lower Bull Street, Birmingham, on the long 104 route from Cannock. (A. B. Cross)

4635 [635 AHA]
Perversely, dual purpose vehicles were used when necessary on town services. 4635 helps out on the Dudley local service D40 when perhaps a double-decker would have been more appropriate. These stylish vehicles might have been built for other B.E.T. operators as 4645 and 4646 were demonstrated to Northern General and Maidstone & District respectively, but no orders were forthcoming. This S15 is in Dudley bus station and is parked in front of B.C.T.'s 2141 [JOJ 141], a 1949 Leyland bodied Leyland PD2/1. (A. B. Cross)

4653 [653 BHA] / 3886 [OHA 886]
Stafford's allocation of single-deckers included examples of all the postwar S types; these were suited to the rural and longer distance routes operated from the town. An almost new B.M.M.O. S14, 4653, with the usual Carlyle-built body on Metal Section frames, shows how the body styles of underfloor-engined postwar single-deck buses had developed. It is parked on Stafford garage yard next to 3886, a Brush bodied dual purpose S13 of 1952 vintage. Although the small radiator grill superficially modernised the appearance of the lightweight S14, the basic concepts in the design are virtually the same. (S. N. J. White)

4656 [656 BHA]
The High Town area of Bridgnorth is a delightful mixture of Elizabethan and Georgian buildings, even having a church designed by Telford, better known for his civil engineering work. Though the old town gate, can be seen in the middle of the main street, the Moot Hall. These were usually built as a town hall-cum-market-cum-gaol. 4656 is being employed on the 909 service from Kidderminster to Wellington. It has yet to be modified and rebuilt as an O.M.O. bus and its Carlyle built 30ft. long body still has a B44F seating configuration. (A. B. Cross)

4660 [660 BHA]
B.M.M.O. S14 4660 is at the top of Castle Hill, Warwick, with the 14th century East Gate to its right. It has just climbed past Warwick Castle and is about to turn into Jury Street. The S14s had begun to displace the 7ft. 6in. wide S6s from about 1961 as 'front line' vehicles and were similarly to have about a twelve year life expectancy. They were the last 30ft. long service buses and were succeeded by the 36ft. long S16s. Both the S14 and S16 classes were built with crash gearboxes, but coupled with the advent of O.M.O., subsequent single-deckers had the more 'driver-friendly' semi-automatic gearboxes. (A. B. Cross)

4671 [671 BHA]
Midland "Red"s 'home-made' S14s developed many variations on the O.M.O./conductor and seating capacity theme during their operational careers. This resulted in very few buses in the class being the same. Perhaps the oddest variation concerned 4671. This bus followed the 1960s craze of having the illuminated advertisement panels that were usually found on double-deckers. 4671 regularly carried the "M & B it's Marvellous Beer" advertisement. However, it rarely seemed to be lit! It is on the 166 route and is leaving Birmingham bus station about 1969. (M. J. Collignon)

4713 [713 BHA]
Stratford-upon-Avon had, for many years, been a focus of Midland "Red"s more southerly routes. Buses from the more marginal parts of the company's operating area were to be seen in the Red Lion bus station. 4713, a 1958 S14, is a good example of this, as it is working the 480 route from Banbury via Shipston-on-Stour. Banbury garage was particularly associated with the S14 class which were well suited to the often rural nature of its operating area. 4713 is in Bridge Foot, on 26/5/1964, near to the late 15th century Clopton Bridge which was named after the Lord Mayor of London of 1492. (G. Pattison)

4722 [722 BHA]
Although 4722 was the prototype thirty-seven seater C5 coach of 1958, it was originally intended to be the last S14 service bus. It had the same integral framework as both the S14 and the S15 classes, but there the similarity ended. It is parked in Digbeth coach station one summer's evening, fairly early in its thirteen-year service life. This five-speed gearbox coach eventually spawned some sixty four other C5 variants. The most famous were the CM5Ts which operated the Birmingham-London service on the M1 motorway. (P. Yeomans)

4723 [723 BHA]
The juxtaposition of B.M.M.O. D7 4723, carrying an advertisement for Atkinsons Bitter and the Cleveland Road Salvation Army Citadel, Wolverhampton, seems a little inappropriate. The date is 21/5/1961 and within a few years much of this scene would have altered or disappeared. Atkinsons had already been taken over by M & B in 1959, the Wolverhampton Corporation trolleybus wires came down in March 1967, while this part of Cleveland Road is now a cul de sac. Behind the M.C.C.W. bodied double-decker is S14 4303, which was also withdrawn that year. (G. Pattison)

4729 [729 BHA]
The last fifty D7s were built in 1957. By this date, manual gearboxes on double-deckers were beginning to go out of favour. The B.M.M.O. constant-mesh gearbox demanded a certain degree of skill and timing and perhaps it was not surprising that these buses were not equipped with an easy change 'box. Certainly, the driver of 4729, with a potential full load on the 133 route to Stourport, might have appreciated such a luxury. The bus is loading on the wrong side of Worcester Street, Birmingham, which was the Bank Holiday loading point for this service. (A. B. Cross)

4732 [732 BHA] / 4021 [SHA 421]
By 1965, Digbeth's overflow site at Benacre Street had been replaced, because of redevelopment, by a yard in Adderley Street, opposite the rear of B.C.T.'s Liverpool Street garage. Adderley Street was something of a 'rough and ready' site, with a rather indifferent surface. The double-deck vehicles here were typical of Digbeth garage's allocation, being D7s and LD8s. The comparison between 4732, a 1959 B.M.M.O. D7, with a M.C.C.W. H37/26R body and 4021, a Leyland PD2/12 with a Leyland H30/26R body of 1953 shows how two manufacturers met the same specification in very different ways. (D. R. Harvey collection)

4738 [738 BHA]
Midland "Red"s services from Birmingham had to parallel B.C.T.'s bus and tram routes in order to reach their destination beyond the city boundary. B.C.T. had the monopoly but, because of 1930s growth, Midland "Red" bus services were sometimes the only public transport from the tram terminus to the boundary. This was the case beyond the Washwood Heath tram terminus on routes which went to Castle Bromwich and Coleshill. 4738 passes Water Orton railway station about 1958 on the 161 route. At that time, Water Orton was a fairly small, isolated village. Today, it is almost surrounded by motorway developments. (A. B. Cross)

4752 [752 BHA]
To reach Bearwood bus station from Bearwood Road, buses travelling from Birmingham, Smethwick and West Bromwich passed the now demolished Bearwood garage and turned right into the short length of Anderson Road, where this photograph was taken. They then used Herbert Road to reach the bus station. The 221 route from West Bromwich was one of these services and is being operated by D7 4752, on what must have been a sunless, but sultry day, as not only are all the ventilation windows open, but so are the doors.   (A. B. Cross)

3467 [MHA 467] & 3232 [JHA 832]
Digbeth had been earmarked in 1940 for widening into a dual carriageway, but this plan was shelved because of World War Two and the site of some of the cleared buildings between the garage and Digbeth was used from 1947 until the mid 1950s to park up to forty five buses. This 1951 view shows an interesting mixture of virtually new vehicles and prewar F.E.D.D. double-deckers. The latter are 2154 and 2251 which are apparently as yet unrebuilt. The new double-decker is Brush bodied D5, 3467, which is in original condition without the driver's windscreen being heightened. Behind it is 3232, a B.M.M.O. S8 with its M.C.C.W. body in original short tailed condition.   (S. E. Letts)

71

BIBLIOGRAPHY

There other books about the Midland "Red" buses which contain further details about the bus fleet, mechanical details and operational events.

Gray, P., Keeley, M., Seale, J. T.P.C. [1978/9] Midland "Red" Volumes 1/2.

Greenwood, M. W. Bradford Barton [1979] Midland "Red" Buses.

Keeley, M. Ian Allan [1983] Midland "Red" Bus Operators 1.

Porter, A. F. Ian Allan [1985] Midlands Buses 1950-1969.

Ian Allan [various] A.B.C. of Midland "Red" Buses & Coaches.

P.S.V. Circle [1959] B.M.M.O. Part II 1934-1959 PD2.

P.S.V. Circle [1961] B.M.M.O. Part I 1904-1933 PD3.